Prediction Techniques
Regarding Romance

Ana Ruiz

ISBN: 0-86690-490-5

Cover Design: Jack Cipolla

First Printing: 1999
Current Printing: 2006

Published by:
American Federation of Astrologers, Inc.
PO Box 22040
6535 S. Rural Road
Tempe, AZ 85285-2040

Printed in the United States of America

Contents

Foreword

My unavailing quest over the years to come across a book dealing only with astrology as it influences the social/romantic life, companioning the drive to get the most out of my personal relationships, has inspired me to write this book.

To know when you may meet a potential lover, when a relationship can go through changes or end, as well as if one is likely to get back together with another are the questions I am most frequently asked.

I will show you how to derive the answers to these type of questions, providing you possess astrological knowledge as well as the complete birth data of the individuals in question.

Several friends and clients have kindly allowed me to publish their relationship experiences as predicted through various branches in astrology. They have been compiled from twelve years of research.

By sharing my studies with you, I can only hope that you are able to gain from them as I have.

Ana Ruiz
Montreal, Canada
1998

Chapter 1

How It Works

*T*he ten planets (including the luminaries—the Sun and Moon) were put in the sky by the creator, a celestial being. The Sun, giver of life, was the first to be born, followed by the rest of the planets. Each planet revolves around the Sun and each stands for a particular human virtue or quality:

- Sun—Will
- Moon—Emotion
- Mercury—Intellect
- Venus—Affection
- Mars—Courage
- Jupiter—Optimism
- Saturn—Perseverance
- Uranus—Originality
- Neptune—Compassion
- Pluto—Cooperation

Spirituality is a combination of acquiring high motives (Sun), refined emotions (Moon), controlled thoughts (Mercury), unselfish affections (Venus) and constructive energies (Mars).

The Sun, being at the center of our Solar System, becomes

a transformer of the planet's energies. These planets then cut the energy field of the Sun as they revolve around it. The planets, while cutting the Sun's enormous energy field, in turn become transformers and transmitters of this energy, depending on the planet which type of energy is transmitted to earth and life on earth. The lines of energy are what we call aspects between the planets.

How the planets were lined up at one's birth date, place and time illustrates the individual's potential. Astrology is a wonderful instrument for learning how and when to make the most of these potentials. A natal or progressed afflicted chart does not indicate negativity in the adverse sense, but shows that it requires more effort and challenges to overcome obstacles in a specific area of life indicated by the houses involved.

Astrology should be used as a tool to make the most out of our potentials and lives. It should not merely be used for predicting, but rather to determine the direction that life is likely to take at a particular time. We can then act accordingly by preparing ourselves to benefit from such directions or learn how to deal with life's obstacles that cross our paths. Astrology also shows us how to improve negative qualities as a result of adverse natal aspects, as the potential lies within each and every one of us to be the best what we can possibly be.

Chapter 2

Venus

*I*n a book such as this, I feel it appropriate to interpret natal Venus through the signs as well as conjunctions received at birth. It can reveal quite a bit about the romantic essence of an individual.

Venus in the Signs

Venus in Aries

Venus in Aries places its own emotional/romantic needs first. Because much self-love comes with this placement, these individuals can be somewhat self-absorbed. The challenge and the chase is what captures their interest. This placement brings the tendency to always make the first move when approaching a romantic interest or potential mate.

Venus in Taurus

Venus in Taurus must own or possess the other person. Physical beauty is an important prerequisite in the choice of partners. Loyalty and emotional security is what this type looks for. The sense of touch is overdeveloped, generating a very sensual lover. Emotions and feelings of affection are long lasting and tend to run deep.

Venus in Gemini

Venus in Gemini needs stimulating intellectual companionship. This type is fond of challenges, flirting and secret liaisons, and enjoys being kept guessing by the other. However this is not the most loyal nor enduring sign for Venus to be placed in. Curiosity and the need for variety and space, characterize this love nature.

Venus in Cancer

Venus in Cancer tends to protect the other person. They have highly sensitive natures requiring reassurance and demonstrative affections to fulfill their strong emotional security needs. Feelings are hard to read as they are kept hidden behind a tough exterior. These individuals are capable of giving and loving with all their heart and soul.

Venus in Leo

Venus in Leo loves to be in love. Each relationship is the love of their life. This individual is very playful, social, demonstrative and loyal, yet is also fond of flirting. The choice of partner must be one that he or she is proud to be seen with. This placing brings a tendency to be ruled by emotions rather than the intellect.

Venus in Virgo

Venus in Virgo is prone to shyness and criticizing the partner. The ideal relationship is sought and never established. Emotions tend to be mentally dissected. Intellectual stimulation is of utmost importance within their relationships. These natives can be somewhat fussy, inhibited or undemonstrative in the romantic expression.

Venus in Libra

Venus in Libra needs to be involved in relationships. This placement generates a very romantic nature. They seek strong intellectual compatibility and physical beauty. The desire to socialize and please the other is highly developed. As with Leo, the choice of romantic partner must be one whom the native is proud to be seen with.

Venus in Scorpio

Venus in Scorpio produces the most physical and passionate type of romantic partner. The nature tends towards suspicion, jealousy, secrecy and revenge once hurt or betrayed. Intense emotional and physical experiences are felt within their relationships. These natives can sometimes confuse love with lust and passion.

Venus in Sagittarius

Venus in Sagittarius displays one who has trouble settling down due to an explorative and fun-loving nature. This type is outspoken and honest. Variety, fun, space and freedom is what they look for in romance. These individuals tend to be attracted to those of foreign countries or backgrounds.

Venus in Capricorn

Venus in Capricorn does not display emotions nor affections, due to a reserved exterior. This type places much emphasis on status and financial security. Frequently, their choice of partners is one of a considerable age difference. This native tends to be concerned with how the relationship appears to others or affects the reputation and social standing.

Venus in Aquarius

Venus in Aquarius is considered the least sexual of all. They tend to love the world and with their minds. What this type looks for is plenty of freedom, spontaneity, excitement and a partner who is a friend first, last and above all. Relationships tend to be somewhat unusual and experimental or end as quickly and suddenly as they begin.

Venus in Pisces

Venus in Pisces will sacrifice or do anything for the object of its affection. This generates the most romantic and sensitive of individuals. Being the last sign, as opposed to Aries the first, this type can love others more than themselves. The love of this individual is unconditional, forgiving and deeply felt.

In order to be compatible, Venus in the charts of two people needs to be configured in one of the examples listed below in order of strength:

- in the same sign, especially within an eight degree orb (conjunction)
- in the same element, within an eight degree orb (trine); for example, one Venus at 14 Leo and the other at 18 Sagittarius.
- in compatible elements, within a six degree orb (sextile); for example, one Venus at 4 Pisces and the other at 9 Taurus

When Venus is harmoniously placed as above, mutual interests and attitudes towards relationships are similar. The manner of expressing affection is alike. These aspects promote understanding and sympathy between people.

When two people have Venus in square or opposition between their charts, minor conflicts or differences result. Attitudes toward social preferences may clash. The manner of expressing affection does not parallel each other.

Venus in the Houses

Venus in the First House

When natal Venus is found in the first house, the individual is the pursuer and initiator when it comes to romantic interests. Individuality is expressed through affections and relationships.

Venus in the Second House

Natal Venus in the second house shows one who seeks to

possess the other. Emphasis is placed on physical appearances due to refined tastes. Finances are subject to improvement through relationships.

Venus in the Third House

Natal Venus in the third house shows one who enjoys talking about every aspect of the current relationship. The individual is fond of communicating affections through telephone, letters, E-mail, etc. An active partner is sought as well as one who is well-informed on many subjects.

Venus in the Fourth House

Natal Venus in the fourth house shows one who enjoys relaxing at home with a partner. As Cancer is the traditional ruler of this house, a partner who acts as a parent figure is usually attracted unless the one with Venus in the fourth house needs to be a parent figure.

Venus in the Fifth House

Natal Venus in the fifth house indicates one who is constantly involved in a relationship. The chosen one must be fond of fifth house pleasures such as dancing, gambling, entertainment and all forms of social recreation.

Venus in the Sixth House

Venus in the sixth house shows one who is rather fussy or picky when it comes to choosing romantic partners. He or she enjoys helping or being of service to the partner. This arises from the sixth house Venus person's need to be needed.

Venus in the Seventh House

Venus in the seventh house indicates one who is always in love, each relationship being "the one." A need to please is always evident with this position. Strong dependence on the partner is usually linked with Venus in the seventh house.

Venus in the Eighth House

Venus in the eighth house reveals intense physical needs based on the highest level of affection. This placement, if well aspected, brings financial or material gains through marriage.

Venus in the Ninth House

Venus in the ninth house brings an interest in those of other cultures. This placement attracts romance while traveling abroad or through learning institutions.

Venus in the Tenth House

Venus in the tenth house shows one who is attracted to those in high positions as well as of a considerable age difference. Relationships established for the purpose of increasing status are likely with this placement.

Venus in the Eleventh House

Venus in the eleventh house shows that the one chosen must be a friend first and foremost. Much emphasis is placed on friendships and group activities. This person tends to be "fixed up" by friends and with friends.

Venus in the Twelfth House

Venus in the twelfth house shows one who is attracted to secret relationships. The danger here is to sacrifice oneself for the other or to select a partner who is helpless and therefore dependent on the twelfth house Venus individual.

Venus Conjunctions

Venus Conjunct Mars

Venus conjunct Mars generates one who is always in pursuit of romance and passionate encounters. The love nature is highly developed. This type is very aware of the potent effect the opposite sex has on them as well as the equally powerful effect they themselves have on the opposite sex. In same-sex relationships, substitute the interpretation with the same sex as opposed to the opposite sex without changing the rest of the delineation.

Venus Conjunct Jupiter

Venus conjunct Jupiter shows one who can be overly generous and optimistic. This type responds well to honesty and frankness. Unless there are contradictions in the chart, this aspect brings a successful and happy marriage.

Venus Conjunct Saturn

Venus conjunct Saturn seeks a partner with a parental image or one who is considerably older, mature or established in life. Affections are cooled down by a down-to-earth nature. Relationships tend to be based upon improving one's social status.

Venus Conjunct Uranus

Venus conjunct Uranus tends to fall in and out of love suddenly. Relationships end as quickly as they begin. This is the classic "love at first sight" aspect. Much social activity is sought, as well as individuals who are somewhat different or unusual.

Venus Conjunct Neptune

Venus conjunct Neptune tends to idealize romantic interests. There is danger of deception through or within their relations as well as the need to escape from the harshness of the world through another, sex or in the relationship itself. This aspect shows a profound ability for spiritual love.

Venus Conjunct Pluto

Venus conjunct Pluto produces profound physical drives and needs. A form of death is experienced when a relationship ends. Power over the object of affection is a requirement which is usually attained through sex.

Analysis of Venus is eminently important and insightful when examining one's romantic/affection potential and tendencies. This is especially relevant when the chart owner has the Sun in Taurus or Libra, or those signs are rising.

Should Venus be found rising before the natal Sun it is known as a morning star. This placement denotes one who is enthusiastic with affections and is hopeful and optimistic in relationships.

Should Venus be found rising after the natal Sun, it is called an evening star. This shows one who is cautious in romantic relationships and is quick to judge and recognize relationship potential in another.

Natal Venus placed in a cardinal sign (Aries, Cancer, Libra, Capricorn) indicates one who initiates romantic encounters and/or opportunities. This individual is not shy and never waits for others to make contact. Particular emphasis is given when placed in the critical degrees of one, thirteen and twenty-six of cardinal signs.

Natal Venus in a fixed sign (Taurus, Leo, Scorpio, Aquarius) denotes one who is loyal, constant, stable and predictable in relationships. This is strongly emphasized when found in either of the critical degrees of nine or twenty-one of fixed signs.

Natal Venus found in a mutable or common sign (Gemini, Virgo, Sagittarius, Pisces) shows one who is changeable, adaptable and versatile when it comes to relationships. Emphasis is given when found in the critical degrees of four and seventeen of mutable signs.

A natal retrograde Venus indicates a "late bloomer" when it comes to matters of the heart. It brings difficulties, however, when expressing or coming to terms with showing true feelings, especially if Venus is found in Aries or Capricorn.

One born with Venus placed in Scorpio, one of the signs of its detriment, tends to have high standards in romantic choices. This individual can be jealous, suspicious and vengeful if other natal indicators reinforce this. If born with Venus in the other sign of its detriment, Aries, the individual is somewhat self-centered and highly values his or her independence. Compromise is on the individual's terms only.

Venus found in its sign of fall, Virgo, shows one who tends to be have very high standards and is critical of romantic partners. Many unmarried or single people have this placement, and remain unattached by choice and due to an analytical romantic nature.

Natal Venus found in its rulership signs, Taurus or Libra, shows one who has strong, healthy emotions and relationships. Venus expresses itself naturally in its own signs.

Venus is most powerful when found in its sign of exaltation, Pisces, especially at twenty-seven degrees. This individual will sacrifice anything for love and has a profound ability to experience love and devotion in relationships.

An intercepted natal Venus indicates one who seeks relationships in a very personal way, keeping them either secret, sacred or hidden from others as well as other areas of life, especially if found in such esoteric signs as Scorpio or Pisces.

Chapter 3

Houses

*T*he fifth house has dominion over love affairs, romance, affections, fun, dating, lovers, social tendencies, pleasures, and relationships (before they become cemented as indicated by the seventh house).

This is the house to observe when deciphering questions related to romantic potential and activity. Should the fifth house contain a planet, it is the fifth house ruler. If more than one planet is found in this house, the one closest to the fifth house cusp is stronger and therefore its primary ruler. The rest of the planets in the fifth house (should there be more than one) are co-rulers and follow in order of strength, judged by how close they are to the fifth house cusp. Should no planets be contained in the fifth house, the planet ruling the sign on the fifth house cusp is the ruler.

Carefully analyze the ruler by sign, house position and natal aspects. Then observe the transits, lunations and progressions.

For example, one with an empty fifth house with Cancer on the cusp, should study the Moon, ruler of Cancer. The Moon in this chart is found in the tenth house. This individual seeks a parent figure or one in high authority with a solid reputation and good standing in the community. It also indicates interest in older, mature and established individuals. The Moon in this chart forms a trine to a second house Venus. This would be interpreted as attraction to one who is financially well off or secure.

In addition, check if transiting Venus is currently making favorable or adverse contacts to planets in or ruling the fifth house.

Transiting Venus through the fifth house augments romantic potential and expands the social life by attracting possible relationships and improving existing ones. This is due to the power of Venus drawing out one's magnetism, charm and appeal. The same applies to transiting Venus forming a favorable aspect to a natal planet in or ruling the fifth house.

Transiting Jupiter through the fifth house brings a strong chance of increased abundance of relationship potential throughout its stay in this house. This is particularly emphasized when a transiting fifth house Jupiter beneficially aspects Venus or a planet in or ruling the fifth house.

Transiting Saturn through the fifth house tends to bring delays and restrictions to matters of the heart. This can be due to a lack of interest or participation in such matters. In an existing relationship, it can manifest as a cooling down of emotions or affections from the partner. Should transiting Saturn make a favorable contact to another planet, especially Venus or a planet in or ruling the fifth house, this activated planet provides clues as to how to release transiting Saturn's restrictions.

Transiting Saturn through the seventh house brings either a test within a committed relationship, restrictions, delays or the end or cementing of a strong relationship. Demands requiring extra effort are then increased within the union. Saturn transiting through the seventh house is a transit of marriage (bonding) as well as of divorce (disintegration).

A friend was experiencing "coldness" in his romantic/social life. Usually popular with the opposite sex, no one seemed to respond to him as they had in the past. Fortunately, toward the end of transiting Saturn's long stay in his fifth house, it was to form a trine to Venus before moving into the sixth house. During that time he met someone and fell in love.

A couple, Craig and Samantha, broke up after dating for about one year. Transiting Saturn was in exact opposition to Samantha's fifth house ruler, severing the ties and dissolving the relationship, as Saturn brings endings and the fifth house ruler points to relationship crisis.

Look to the seventh house for insight into relationships in which two people have made a commitment to each other as opposed to just dating each other as seen by the fifth house. The fifth house represents the lover while the seventh house represents the spouse or the equivalent. Transits, lunations and progressions formed to this house ruler (which is established in the same manner) provide the insight required to forecast a serious, cemented relationship.

The twelfth house stands for limitations and the end of a love affair. Transits, lunations and progressions formed to this house ruler can bring on such an event. This twelfth house is the eighth house (of losses and endings) from the fifth house of romance.

Tara has an empty fifth house. Mercury, this house's ruler, forms an opposition to her twelfth house Saturn. Several relationships of hers have ended when a transit or lunation adversely aspected Mercury and/or Saturn. Natal Saturn in the twelfth house brings extreme depression when a relationship fails and terminates.

The most recent transit of this type she experienced prompted a break-up when transiting Saturn was in exact square to her natal twelfth house Saturn. It is an aspect of challenge, tests, crisis and losses.

Saturn has a way of drawing out what is wrong in marriage

or a relationship in order for it to be confronted and resolved. Should it not pass the test, the union will outgrow itself and die. Its time has come.

There are various ways of interpreting Saturn through the seventh house—transits, lunations and progressions—all of which will direct you toward the correct interpretation. However, conclusions should not be made until the charts of both individuals have been fully analyzed.

Tara and Sean broke up on the day transiting Mercury, ruler of her fifth house, formed a square to her seventh house Moon (emotions within a relationship). Neptune, ruler of his empty fifth house, formed by transit a square to his exact Saturn-seventh house conjunction. In addition, transiting Venus and Mars were both forming an opposition to her seventh house cusp (Descendant/relationships).

Two people involved in a relationship approaching transits of this nature at the same time guarantees a time coming where extreme caution should be taken to prevent the relationship from terminating should other transits show the possibility of hope. If non-existent, a break up is more than likely.

Chapter 4

Derivative Houses

*A*s we have seen, we tend to attract relationships or romance when Venus transits through the fifth and seventh houses. Venus brings out one's charm and magnetism when in these houses. However, romance can be found in all twelve houses—you just have to know where and how to look!

By using derivative houses (reading other people's houses through your own chart), a wealth of new information can be attained which may have otherwise been overlooked. For example, when Venus transits through your sixth house, not only can you attract an office romance (sixth house) but you may also meet someone interesting and develop a relationship by attending a get-together at the home (fourth house) of an neighbor or eldest sibling (third house).

When using derivative houses, place the house in question, being the third house ruling neighbors and siblings in the above example, in the first house position. Then your sixth house is the fourth house of the neighbor or sibling.

A thorough knowledge of what each of the twelve houses rule is essential when using derivative houses. By observing

Venus as it transits the houses of your chart, you may attract romance in many different situations described through this chapter by reading other people's charts through your own.

First House

Traditional: By being outgoing and initiating social activities; by expressing yourself in a positive manner through activities involving self-improvement; or through connections or dealings with grandparents.

Derivative: Through or with the eldest sibling or neighbor of a friend (first house is the third house from the eleventh house); with or through a friend of a neighbor or eldest sibling (first house is the eleventh house from the third house); with or through associates, advisors, business partners of the third eldest sibling (first house is the seventh house from the seventh house); or at the home of a boss, employer or parent (first house is the fourth house from the tenth house).

Second House

Traditional: Through financial institutions; while making purchases; or through dealings with music, art or luxury items.

Derivative: Through long travels or learning institutions related to work (second house is the ninth house from the sixth); at the home of friends (second house is the fourth house from the eleventh); through friends of the family (second house is the eleventh house from the fourth house); through the parent of a friend (second house is the fourth house from the eleventh house); through or with the boss or employer of your first child (second house is the tenth house from the fifth house) or through connections with step-brothers (second house is the fifth house from the tenth house).

Third House

Traditional: Through correspondence, advertising or phone calls; through short travels, commuting or ground transportation; through connections with the eldest sibling; through or with a neighbor; or through schooling or classes.

Derivative: Through connections with children of friends (third house is the fifth house from the eleventh); by traveling with an associate or business partner (third house is the ninth house from the seventh house) through or with a parent of a co-worker (third house is the tenth house from the sixth house); through the parent's work (third house is the sixth house from the tenth house) or socializing or at a party with friends (third house is the fifth house from the eleventh house).

Fourth House

Traditional: Through family contacts; within the home environment or get-togethers in the home; or through dealings with land developments and real estate.

Derivative: Through or with a friend of a co-worker (fourth house is the sixth house from the eleventh house); groups or clubs related to work (fourth house is the eleventh house from the sixth house); through the business partner or spouse of your boss (fourth house is the seventh house from the tenth house) or through or with the co-worker of a friend (fourth house is the sixth house from the eleventh house).

Fifth House

Traditional: Through activities involving fun and entertainment; through matters dealing with children and creativity; by attending concerts, shows, museums or casinos; through socializing at parties; while on holidays; by attending nightclubs, theaters or schools; by participating in games; and through connections with the second eldest sibling.

Derivative: Through connections with a friend's business partner or spouse (fifth house is the seventh house from the eleventh house); while on short trips or commuting with a neighbor or eldest sibling (fifth house is the third house from the third house) or through friends of a business partner or associate (fifth house is the eleventh house from the seventh house).

Sixth House

Traditional: Through work or a co-worker; through institutions dealing with health and diet; at a restaurant; through connections with an aunt or uncle; through or with a tenant; by participating in volunteer activities or at a clothing store.

Derivative: At the home of a neighbor or eldest sibling (sixth house is the fourth house from the third house); while on a business trip in a foreign land (sixth house is the tenth house from the ninth house); through connections or with a neighbor of a parent (sixth house is the third house from the fourth house) or through or with a neighbor's parent (sixth house is the fourth house from the third house).

Seventh House

Traditional: Through or with counselors, advisors and others; through or with business partners or associates; through connections or activities with grandparents; through connections or activities with your second child or third eldest sibling.

Derivative: Through the lover of your eldest sibling or neighbor (seventh house is the fifth house from the third house); through long distance travel with friends (seventh house is the ninth house from the eleventh house) or through connections or activities involving nieces and nephews (seventh house is the fifth house from the third house).

Eighth House

Traditional: Through matters of the occult; activities involving inheritances, legacies and the death of others; of a secretive nature or through matters involving funerals.

Derivative: Through or with the co-worker of a sibling or neighbor (eighth house is the sixth house from the third house); through connections with the friends of your parents (eighth house is the 11th house from the tenth house); through connections with a friend's parents (eighth house is the tenth house from the 11th house); through or with the siblings of co-workers (eighth house is the third house from the sixth house) or through connections involving step-brothers or step-sisters (eighth house is the fifth house from the fourth house).

Ninth House

Traditional: Through colleges, universities and other institutions of higher learning; through long distance travel; through religious or spiritual matters or connections; with an individual of a different culture; on airplanes; through connections with the fourth eldest sibling or third child; or through a dis*tance*.

Derivative: Through connections or with the friend of a friend (ninth house is the eleventh house from the eleventh house); through or with a co-worker of a parent (ninth house is the sixth house from the fourth house); through the spouse or partner of the eldest sibling or neighbor (ninth house is the seventh house from the third house); or through connections or activities with your grandchildren (ninth house is the fifth house from the fifth house).

Tenth House

Traditional: Through the career, through or with a boss or employer; through connections with the parents; with an older individual; through those or with someone of authority and status; or through a promotion.

Derivative: Through connections with the children of a co-worker (tenth house is the fifth house from the sixth house); through connections with a parent's business partner or associate (tenth house is the seventh house from the fourth house); or through connections with a cousin (tenth house is the fifth house from the sixth house).

Eleventh House

Traditional: Through participating in clubs, groups or organizations; through friends, or by a friend becoming more than that.

Derivative: Through connections with a business partner's children (eleventh house is the fifth house from the seventh house); through connections with the marriage partner of the second eldest sibling (eleventh house is the seventh house from the fifth house); through connections with the lover or business partner of an associate or advisor (eleventh house is the fifth house from the seventh house); through long distance travels with the eldest sibling or neighbor (eleventh house is the ninth house from the third house); or by dining out with a co-worker (eleventh house is the sixth house from the sixth house).

Twelfth House

Traditional: Through places of confinement, such as hospitals, prisons and rehabilitation centers; of a secretive nature; through medical or religious institutions, or through charitable institutions.

Derivative: Through the neighbor or eldest sibling of your boss or employer (twelfth house is the third house from the tenth house); through connections with an aunt or uncle (twelfth house is the third house from the tenth house); through connections with the spouse of a co-worker (twelfth house is the seventh house from the sixth house); or through long distance travels with a parent (twelfth house is the ninth house from the fourth house).

Chapter 5

Transits

*T*ransits formed to the individual charts of two people involved provide an immense source of information regarding the direction the relationship is most likely to take. The outer planets, (Jupiter through Pluto) are the most indicative of major changes, events or adjustments within the relationship as their motion is longer and therefore much more effective and noticeable.

When observing transits, the Ptolemaic aspects work best and provide the most data—conjunction, opposition, square, trine and sextile. Orbs allowed in transits are smaller than those used in natal astrology. An orb of five degrees is most effective.

Venus

A square or opposition brings challenges and struggles. When an outer planet forms either aspect to natal Venus, representing the relationship, a test or crisis must be confronted within the union.

Transiting Venus conjunct or trine natal Mercury can manifest as encountering a relationship through Mercury-related activities such as work and travel.

A favorable transit from Venus to itself or the ruler of the fifth or seventh house improves an existing relationship or introduces a new one providing one is single and looking. Natal Venus is favorably activated by transiting Venus being in the same sign or element attracting others to you. Transiting Venus through the natal Sun sign also increases romantic potential by drawing out magnetism, appeal and popularity.

Mars

Natal Mars being favorably aspected by transiting Venus combines the elements of affection and attraction, resulting in a more active social/romantic life.

Adverse aspects involving these two planets can bring obstacles, impulsiveness, challenges and even break-ups. This transit has been known to bring about relationships based on physical needs alone.

Active Mars by transit can bring about a relationship if it well aspects Venus (romance) or the ruler of the fifth house (relationship) or the seventh house (commitment).

A negative transit (square or opposition) between Mars and the Sun in a female chart, or Mars and the Moon in a male chart, tends to result in arguments and disagreements within the relationship. Mars represents repressed anger while the Sun represents the man in the life of a female chart to which it is directed. The Moon or Venus represents the woman in the life of a male chart to whom the anger or disagreement is directed towards.

Tina and Kyle separated after living together for several years. Kyle needed space. Tina was devastated. At this time, transiting Venus and Mars were both squaring her natal Mars. This aspect brought emotional barriers and conflicts within the relationship to attention. Mars, planet of tension and arguments was being activated by transiting Venus (relationships) as well as by transiting Mars, negatively by the square.

Fortunately, months later he moved back in and they are still living happily together along with a beautiful baby daughter. In effect when they reunited were transiting Venus trine her natal Sun, Mercury and Venus. Three personal planets were being activated by transiting Venus. Venus aspecting her Sun brought about mutual understanding and agreement within the relationship. Activated Mercury increased her level of comprehension and communication resulting in calm, clear conversations. Lastly, transiting Venus trine Venus brought the harmony, sympathy, understanding and forgiveness required to resume the relationship.

In Kyle's chart, transiting Mars was conjunct his Venus. His feelings of love and affection within this relationship (Venus) were activated by Mars, planet of activity and action, triggering the reunion.

Jupiter

Natal Jupiter being transited by Venus is a most auspicious and rewarding time for romance, dating and relationships. Jupiter is the planet of luck, abundance and opportunity. When these two fortunate planets align and form a trine, sextile or conjunction you can anticipate a romantically rewarding experience. A square or opposition between these two planets can bring setbacks arising from unhealthy excessive indulgences, including extramarital or romantic activity.

Transiting Jupiter well aspected to Venus is similar to transiting Venus to Jupiter, only it lasts much longer in time due to Jupiter's slower movement.

Saturn

Transits of Saturn either stabilize/cement or end/terminate relationships. Either way, tests and challenges must be dealt with and confronted. Saturn also rules older people, the past, reunions, disruptions and separations.

Observe what Saturn is doing by transit to the charts of two people involved. Should it square or oppose both people's

Suns at the same time, trouble can be expected. If Saturn is retrograde by transit, the reversal or setback can be temporary.

Nikki and Roger dated for two years before he moved in with her. Just two weeks later, he left and moved out. At this time, transiting Saturn was squaring her seventh house Venus and twelfth house Uranus, co-ruler of her seventh house.

Transiting Saturn square her natal seventh house Venus brought considerable tension and trouble to the relationship, not only because Saturn aspects Venus negatively, but more because Venus is found in the seventh house of relationships. This is known as a classic break-up transit. Under these influences, affections seem to cool down and at worst dissolve altogether. Interest in maintaining the relationship may disappear, resulting in a rude awakening. However, a good, healthy, solid relationship will survive the tests and challenges and emerge as a stronger union.

If one is experiencing this transit or an opposition and is not involved in a relationship, it is best to focus on other areas of life as love is now particularly hard to find.

Transiting Saturn was also in square to Nikki's Uranus, co-ruler of her seventh house of relationships. This is another transit of great tension. Saturn brings restrictions and rigidity while Uranus seeks freedom, change and independence. These two aspects were clashing with each other at the time of the separation, especially as the two planets (Venus an Uranus) are strongly connected with her seventh house as ruler and co-ruler.

Transiting Saturn favorably aspecting one's natal Venus can rekindle or reactivate a past romance. As Saturn rules older people as well as those from the past, a favorable transit from Venus will activate such events in your life.

Saturn is a karmic planet, and when it transits to align with natal Venus it can bring a fated relationship into one's life. An opposition between transiting Saturn and natal Venus is sure to shake up a relationship. If it has outgrown its purpose it will come to an end. However, if it survives, the enormous challenges brought on by the opposition will solidify it.

Transiting Saturn favorably aspecting the ruler of the fifth or seventh house may also reactivate a past romance, especially if Saturn is currently in retrograde motion or resumes its direct course after having been retrograde during the break-up. Like Venus, transiting Saturn favorably aspecting the ruler of the fifth or seventh house can also cement a relationship into a deeper commitment.

When Sean left Tara, transiting Saturn was not only conjunct his Venus, cooling his emotions towards her, but was also trine her Venus, increasing her feelings of affection toward him. However, transiting Saturn was also square her natal Saturn while it was trine her natal Venus. Saturn square Saturn is a powerful transit bringing tests, challenges, increased responsibilities and lessons which need to be learned. In Tara's natal chart we find Venus and Saturn connected by an inconjunct aspect. The trine between Venus and Saturn by transit was strongly overpowered by the square between Saturn and transiting Saturn as Venus and Saturn are natally adversely aspected in Tara's chart.

The effects of transiting Venus to natal Saturn are similar, yet pass much more quickly due to Venus' faster motion. Transiting Venus favorably aspecting natal Saturn can also rekindle a past romance. Craig and Samantha got back together for several weeks when transiting Sun and Venus were sextile her natal Saturn. However, it lasted only a few weeks until they broke up permanently under transiting Venus conjunct her natal Saturn. This transit forced her to see things as they really were, courtesy of Saturn's sobering influence.

Uranus

Transits of Uranus to Venus or the ruler of the fifth or seventh house can bring sudden, unusual and exciting relationships. Uranus triggers the need for excitement through what is considered to be unconventional in the form of quick, abrupt and often unstable and unexpected events.

Transiting Uranus conjunct Venus brings sensational effects. A need for change arises in existing relationships. One may encounter another who is very much different from others in the past. Opportunities emerge for new and exciting relationships under the transiting sextile and trine between these two planets. A square or opposition can be unpredictable and disturbing. Differences between the two people involved are then strained. It marks a period of readjustment. Unstable unions are sure to dissolve under these transits. A new relationship commencing under such transits is not destined to last or be solid or trustworthy.

Transiting Venus aspecting natal Uranus produces similar effects only not as long in duration due to Venus's faster motion.

Dan and Christine broke up under transiting Mars conjunct her natal Uranus. This is an aspect of sudden tension, abrupt behavior and the unexpected. Also operating at the same time was transiting Venus conjunct her natal Saturn.

Dan and Christine got back together for a few months when transiting Venus was conjunct his natal Saturn, a transit promoting reunions and encounters with those from the past. A similar transit was in effect in Christine's chart—transiting Sun was sextile her Saturn. Saturn, planet of the past, was being triggered by transits to both their charts, bringing them back together. However, they split up for the last time when transiting Venus opposed her natal Saturn, effectuating the termination of the relationship.

Transiting Uranus was in retrograde motion and conjunct Tina's natal Sun, her chart ruler with Leo rising, causing a sudden change in her relationship with Kyle when he moved out of their home.

Transits of Uranus, especially to Venus or a planet in or ruling the fifth or seventh house, can bring sudden infatuations. There is also the danger of being indiscreet. The need for a change as well as independence in relationships is greatly emphasized under Uranus transits.

Neptune

Transiting Neptune well aspected to natal Venus or the planet in or ruling the fifth or seventh house can bring a soul mate into one's life. Neptune is the planet of romance, imagination and spirituality.

Adverse aspects tend to introduce an element of deception, illusion, confusion, trickery, secrecy, unreliability or dishonesty to a relationship. Transiting Neptune was squaring Tina's Mars when her relationship fell apart. This is a transit of defeat which forces one to confront issues.

Transiting Venus aspecting Neptune has the same significance, only of much shorter duration due to Venus' quicker motion.

Pluto

Pluto, like Saturn, can bring a renewal of passions if favorably aspected by transit to Venus or a planet in or ruling the fifth or seventh house. Pluto can awaken deep and intense hidden feelings as well as intensifying physical needs within a relationship.

Existing relationships experience a cycle of change, regrowth and development under such transits.

Adverse transits of Pluto can dissolve a relationship due to power struggles, need for control, possessiveness and jealousy. Pluto can also introduce an element of manipulation, un-cooperation or, at worst, cruelty and/or violence into a relationship.

Pluto has a way of eliminating what is not conducive to growth within a relationship. Negative transits can cause a relationship to outlive itself. Favorable transits can result in a rebirth within the relationship.

Transiting Venus aspecting Pluto has similar effects, however they pass much more quickly due to Venus' faster motion.

Chapter 6

Synastry

*T*he word "synastry" comes from the Greek *synastria*, meaning similarity (*syn*) of the stars (*astria*). In Webster's dictionary, "syn" is defined as a prefix meaning "together" or "at the same time."

Synastry is the astrological art of chart comparison between two people. Both horoscopes are compared, analyzed and interpreted in terms of compatibility potential.

A myriad of fine books on this topic exist. However, I will briefly state some of the most important synastric aspects.

In Carl Jung's *Synchroninty*, he states the best cross aspects to have between two charts are one's Sun, Moon and/or Ascendant conjunct or opposing the other's Sun, Moon and/or Ascendant. These have been statistically proven to be the best synastric aspects. Top priority was given to one's Sun conjunct the other's Moon.

These aspects in synastry deliver emotional understanding between the two people combined with an element of mutual cooperation and respect. Personalities integrate well while complimenting the other's as similar traits are found and therefore balanced within each other.

When one's Sun, Moon and/or Ascendant conjuncts or opposes the partner's Sun, Moon and/or Ascendant it results in a powerful connection or combination involving the blending of personalities (Sun), emotions (Moon) and individualities (Ascendant).

Research has also proven that Venus and Mars play a significant yet somewhat secondary role in terms of importance in synastry. These two planets have romantic/sexual relevance. Venus activates affections/emotions while Mars triggers desire and physical attraction/needs.

Cross aspects between one's Venus and the other's Mars are significantly compatible and therefore rewarding and successful to the relationship. This is emphasized when one partner's Mars and the other partner's Venus are found in the same sign or at least in the same element (both in fire, earth, water or air signs).

Compatibility between Venuses (both in same sign or element) is one of the best synastric cross aspects, particularly if both Venuses are within an eight degree orb forming a conjunction or trine. Such a cross aspect activates romantic attraction while triggering affection within each other. Romantic tendencies and interests are similar, therefore increasing the compatibility level.

Should no synastric ties be found within two charts, attraction is unlikely or at least short-lived. A cross aspect between one's Saturn (planet of longevity) and another's personal planet (Sun, Moon, Mercury, Venus and/or Mars) helps the relationship to progress, stabilize and endure.

Another excellent aspect to possess between two charts in synastry is to have the ruler of one's Ascendant ruling the Descendant sign of the other and vice versa.

Tara's chart ruler is Uranus (Aquarius rising) and her Sun is found in Leo on the seventh house cusp. Her current partner, David, has Leo rising with Uranus, ruler of his seventh house in Leo, Tara's Sun sign and seventh house ruler. These are very promising cross aspects for two people involved to have.

In the chart of a female, the location of the Sun and Mars reveal the qualities or traits that attract her. The sign, house position and aspects formed to the Sun and Mars are to be considered, analyzed and interpreted.

In the chart of a male, the Moon and Venus are to be studied to determine the type of individual one is attracted to.

For example, a female with the Sun in Scorpio and Mars in Pisces seeks one who is tenacious, secretive, sexual, emotional and introspective (Scorpio), as well as responsible, receptive, romantic, sympathetic, self-sacrificing and spiritual (Pisces).

A male with the Moon in Virgo and Venus in Capricorn would be attracted to another who is emotionally practical, analytical, reserved and dependable (Virgo) as well as conservative, cautious, undemonstrative and faithful (Capricorn).

Chapter 7

Retrogrades

A retrograde planet appears to move backwards through the zodiac. When it stops this motion, it is said to be stationary. When it resumes its direct course, it is said to be in direct motion. A transiting stationary planet exactly apsecting a natal planet is increased in strength.

All planets move in retrograde motion except the luminaries—the Sun and Moon. A retrograde planet can touch the same point as often as three times within its retrograde cycle.

Mercury retrogrades about three times each year and usually in the same element. Venus turns retrograde about every one and a half years, while Mars goes retrograde about every two years. The outer planets (Jupiter through Pluto) remain retrograde for months a time.

Break-ups are more common under an adverse retrograde aspect. On the other hand, reunions are just as common when the planet resumes its direct course.

When Mercury turns retrograde by transit, expect communication breakdowns and misunderstandings. This is emphasized if Mercury transits through the fifth or seventh house or if one is born under the signs of Gemini or Virgo (Sun or Ascendant) as both share Mercury as their ruler. However, one born under a retrograde Mercury can experience a time of heightened awareness, comprehension and intuition when Mercury goes retrograde.

Should problems exist within a relationship, do your best to resolve them before Mercury goes retrograde. Otherwise this could bring a time of miscommunication and misinterpretation. Avoid verbally reconciling with another under a retrograde Mercury cycle. Wait for it to resume its direct motion for improved communications.

When Venus goes retrograde by transit, relationships can be subject to reversals. A separation under a retrograde Venus cycle may be inconclusive and a reunion is possible when Venus goes direct. This is emphasized if Venus rules the fifth or seventh house, as well as if one is born under Taurus or Libra (Sun or Ascendant) as both signs share Venus as their ruler.

Use transiting Venus in retrograde motion to closely re-evaluate existing problems within a relationship. This is a time when we look back and re-assess our relationships. A romance begun during a Venus retrograde cycle is usually one that existed previously or is one that will be wrought with problems if confirmed by other transits. The romantic expression during this time is generally blocked or inhibited. Transiting Venus retrograde through the natal fifth house in particular can bring a romance back into your life that never fulfilled its destiny or purpose. The same applies to the seventh house only the relationship was more deeply committed and long term. In existing relationships, problems may resurface under a Venus retrograde that were not fully dealt with previously.

Should a break-up occur under an adverse Venus transit, a retrograde Venus by transit can bring the person back into your life.

Retrograde aspects should not be analyzed alone. The quality of the transits and lunations operating at the same time will either confirm or nullify its effects.

Daryl broke up with Melanie when transiting retrograde Venus crossed his Descendant, affecting the relationship (seventh house). Weeks later, when Venus transited by retrograde to the same point, he received a phone call from her. However, they did not reunite as transiting Saturn (restrictions, delays) was in opposition to his natal Venus (relationship) throughout the break-up. Transiting Jupiter was also in opposition to the ruler of his fifth house (romance) ruler.

Chapter 8

Progressions

*P*rogressions have always provided valuable insight into relationship potentials and directions. A one degree orb is allowed when you count ahead the number in years from the birthdate GMT.

Progressed aspects resulting in increased romantic activity, such as introducing a new relationship, include aspects that are formed to natal Venus or a planet in or ruling the fifth or seventh house. The progressed Moon aspecting (conjunction being the strongest) natal Venus tends to bring a new romance.

Progressed Venus making a favorable contact (especially a conjunction) to a planet in or ruling the first, fifth or seventh house brings a romantically rewarding cycle.

Other aspects to anticipate include the progressed Moon conjunct the natal Sun, progressed Sun conjunct the natal Moon or a planet in or ruling the fifth or seventh house.

The Ascendant and Midheaven can also be progressed to see if they make a conjunction (or favorable aspect) by progression to Venus or a planet in or ruling the first, fifth or seventh house.

In the chart of a female, observe the progressions formed to the natal Sun and Mars as well as the aspects formed by the progressed Sun and Mars to the natal planets to determine when one is under a favorable romantic progression cycle.

In the chart of a male, to determine romantic potential, analyze the progressions formed to the Moon and Venus as well as the aspects made by the progressed Moon and Venus to natal planets.

Compare one person's progressed planet to see how it aspects the natal or progressed planet of another. It would be ideal for timing as well as compatibility to have one's progressed Sun, Moon or Venus conjunct or trine the other's natal or progressed Sun, Moon or Venus at the same time.

A progressed aspect within one degree from the ruler or a planet in the seventh house must exist in order to bring about marriage or its equivalent (with the exception of the progressed Moon, due to its changeable and inconstant nature). Relationships cemented or marriages formed while the progressed Moon travels through one's seventh house seldom last as a result of the Moon's rapid motion. The progressed Moon traveling through the natal fifth house can bring an emotional need for romance or induce changes within an existing relationship.

Observe the aspects the progressed Moon makes each month as it forms sensitive angles to the natal chart. The progressed Moon, when combined with transits and lunations, acts as a triggering device for the major progressions.

Tara met Sean when her progressed Moon opposed her natal seventh house Venus. They broke up a year later when the progressed Moon opposed her seventh house Uranus. Tara's previous relationship ended when the progressed Moon made an inconjunct aspect to her natal seventh house Uranus, also her chart ruler.

Chapter 9

Void-of-Course Moon

*W*hen the Moon is in this state it is placed between its last major aspect and its ingress into the next sign. Once again, only the Ptolemaic aspects apply. It can last as little as a few minutes or as long as a few days.

The effect of a void-of-course Moon can be interpreted as a retrograde Moon cycle. Plans initiated and decisions made at this time do not turn out as anticipated. It is as if the event is not receiving any lunar energy and therefore does not reach its desired goal.

The void-of-course Moon tends to produce unrealistic plans based on faulty judgment or delusions. These events are usually abandoned once the Moon makes a major aspect in its new sign.

Misunderstandings are common under this lunar energy, or rather, lack of energy. This cycle is best used for inner repair work, reflection, meditation and sticking to routine.

A relationship beginning under a void-of-course Moon will lack endurance unless other factors in the chart contradict this. On the other hand, a break-up under this lunar cycle may not be permanent.

If you are hoping to get back together with an ex-lover do not initiate plans or contact under such a Moon. The results will be inconclusive and a waste of time and emotional energy. Wait until the Moon moves into the next sign and makes a favorable contact to a natal planet before initiating plans and decisions.

Whenever possible, do not to schedule or agree to go on a first date while the Moon is void-of-course. On the other hand, if you are trying to end a relationship, this lunar condition may not bring about the permanent ending originally desired.

Tara wished to get back together with Sean after they broke up. She arranged a meeting with him, they met and it seemed to her like they were on hopeful ground. The next days, filled with optimism, she waited and waited for him to call and the call never came. When she consulted my advice, I asked her for the exact date and time when they briefly reunited. A quick look at the ephemeris showed me the Moon was void of course throughout that day and night. They never did communicate with each other again.

Chapter 10

Lunations

*L*unations are among my favorite tools within astrology as so much knowledge can be gained through this method.

A new Moon is a conjunction of the transiting Sun and Moon. Its influence lasts one month, until the next new Moon. On occasion, two new Moons can occur in the same month, the second being known as a Blue Moon.

A new Moon is fortunate in terms of romance when it falls in the natal fifth or seventh house (relationships) of one's chart. The same applies when the new Moon conjuncts Venus or the planet in or ruling the fifth or seventh house affecting the romantic life. This lunation promotes growth an opportunities. A five degree orb is allowed between lunations and natal planets.

A new Moon forming a sextile aspect to natal Saturn, planet of reunions, can bring a reconciliation between separated lovers. Should the new Moon trine a natal planet in the fifth house of love affairs, or its ruling planet, a new romance is likely initiated or the improvement of an existing one can be anticipated.

A new Moon in the third house of communication forming a sextile to a natal (or transiting) planet in or ruling the fifth house is the best time to come to mutual agreements or correct past misunderstandings within a troubled relationship.

A new Moon in the fifth house of romance forming a trine aspect to a natal or transiting planet in the first house or to its ruling planet can also activate a new relationship as well as re-kindling a past romance. The same can be expected with a seventh house (relationship) new Moon transit in sextile to a planet in or ruling the fifth house of love affairs.

A new Moon through the seventh house of relationships forming a trine to a natal or transiting planet in the third house (of communications) or to its ruler can improve verbal contact and increase understanding between two people involved. It can also reactivate a recently terminated relationship due to increased or improved communications leading to re-conciliations.

A new Moon in the ninth house (foreign lands/long distance travel) forming a trine to a natal or transiting planet in the fifth house or to its ruler, can bring a romance either with someone of another nationality or while traveling abroad (in reference to where one resides).

A new Moon in the twelfth house (of the past) forming an inconjunct to a natal or transiting planet in or ruling the fifth house can also bring back a past love.

A new Moon if in opposition to Venus or a planet in or ruling the fifth or seventh house is not as fortunate as a conjunction.

Tina and Kyle broke up when the new Moon opposed her Descendant. Months later, they reunited when the new Moon trined her Venus and Mars. The same New Moon was conjunct Kyle's Neptune, ruler of his seventh house, when they got back together.

A full Moon, the opposition between transiting Sun and Moon, has an influence for two weeks, until the next new

Moon. A five degree orb is also applied here.

This lunation brings closure and matters out into the open. Impulsiveness or hasty action taken at this time can bring relationship reversals or undo recent progress made in this area. Setting plans into motion and forming new beginnings is not recommended under full Moon influences.

A full Moon forming a conjunction or opposition to Venus, Saturn or the planet in or ruling the fifth or seventh house can sever romantic ties or bring difficulties requiring attention or adjustment. However, the charts of both people must be affected by this lunation in order for it to materialize within the relationship.

A full Moon in the first house can bring a break-up due to a lack of compromising as it also opposes the seventh house of relationships. This is further emphasized if the full Moon negatively aspects another natal planet, mainly Venus, Saturn or a planet in or ruling the fifth or seventh house.

A full Moon in the romance houses, the fifth and seventh, can also terminate relationships as this lunation has a detrimental effect on the area (house) in which it falls by transit. Specifically, if the lunation adversely aspects natal Venus, Saturn or a planet in or ruling the fifth or seventh house.

When Tina and Kyle broke up, the full Moon at the time was forming an opposition to his twelfth house Venus.

Tara's relationship ended when the full Moon was in her fifth house and also forming a square to her seventh house Moon.

Christine and Dan split up when the full Moon was conjunct her seventh house chart ruler. The same lunation was also forming a conjunction to his Saturn, cooling his affections. They got back together for several months, only to break up permanently when the full Moon was conjunct Christine's Saturn and Dan's South Node.

Roger moved out of Nikki's home when the full Moon not

only formed a conjunction to her fourth house (home/domestic relations) Neptune, but also a square to her seventh house Venus and twelfth house (endings/separations) Uranus. Nikki's Venus and Uranus were also being squared by transiting Saturn at the time of the break up.

Chapter 11

Eclipses

*A*t least two and as many as four solar eclipses occur an-
nually. The effects are beneficial and can last up to one
year. Transits and lunations are to be used as timing devices to
see when the eclipse is triggered.

A solar eclipse falling in your fifth house will bring an activated social/romantic life. The Sun is then in its natural
house, stirring up the need to express yourself through relationships and affections. The same interpretation applies to a
solar eclipse conjunct natal Venus or a planet in or ruling the
fifth or seventh house.

A solar eclipse transiting through your seventh house also
activates relationship potential and opportunities. However,
these relationships are more significant or serious than those
of a fifth house nature. A solar eclipse in the seventh house is
an excellent time for weddings.

Samantha was proposed to during a solar eclipse conjunct
her fifth house ruler. However, to her it was a fifth house type
relationship and she was not ready to commit to a more serious, permanent level with this man.

A solar eclipse opposing Venus or a planet in or ruling the

fifth or seventh house has an adverse affect on romance. It indicates a time of great caution in preventing relationship problems from arising.

A lunar eclipse has a weakening and negative effect during its six-month influence. Between two and four lunar eclipses take place each year. Transits and lunations trigger the effects and provide us with the timing of the events.

A lunar eclipse falling in the fifth or seventh house can bring rejection from a romantic interest as well as delays, setbacks and upsetting changes in existing relationships throughout its stay in this house. I have seen many relationships fall apart under this influence. The same interpretation is applied to the transiting lunar eclipse conjunct or opposite natal Venus or a planet in or ruling the fifth or seventh house.

Tara and Sean broke up when the lunar eclipse opposed her seventh house Moon. It took place three months before the actual break-up, however the triggering aspects are illustrated throughout this book. The same eclipse was in opposition to his Pluto, ruler of the house holding his seventh house ruler.

Tara broke up with a previous boyfriend years earlier when the lunar eclipse was in opposition to her seventh house Pluto. The solar eclipse operating at the same time was also in opposition to her seventh house Moon, severing the ties.

Craig and Samantha broke up when the lunar eclipse opposed her seventh house Venus, separating her from her lover.

However, by knowing in advance through astrology when problems can arise we are able to overcome difficulties if the relationship is meant to be.

Under a lunar eclipse in the above mentioned conditions, extra care should be taken by increasing levels of understanding, cooperation, communication, trust, compromise and caution between two people involved during the critical dates triggered by transits and lunations.

Chapter 12

Arabian Parts

*A*lso known as Arabic Points or Lots, they come to us from medieval Arabia. Many believe this system to go as far back as the ancient Babylonians and Egyptians. A book written by 10th century Arabic astrologer al-Biruni titled *The Book of Instruction in the Elements of the Art of Astrology* lists the many Arabic parts with their calculation and explanations. There are over 150 Arabian Parts to work with that can provide much insight into the chart. Transits, lunations and progressions activate the potentials of these points. The most common Arabian Part is the Part of Fortune; however we will now work with points directed towards relationship queries.

Use the following table to convert these placings into a workable number within the 360° Zodiac:

Aries	0-29
Taurus	30-59
Gemini	60-89
Cancer	90-119
Leo	120-149
Virgo	150-179
Libra	180-209

Scorpio	210-239
Sagittarius	240-269
Capricorn	270-299
Aquarius	300-329
Pisces	330-359

To find the Arabic Part of Love, add the Ascendant to Venus and subtract the Sun.

Example: Asc. 20 Aquarius	=	300 + 20 = 320
+Venus 18 Cancer	=	90 + 18 = 108
- Sun 9 Gemini	=	60 + 9 = 69
= Part of Love 29 Pisces	=	330 + 29 = 359

Should you arrive at a final figure of 360° or more, simply subtract 360° and this is your Part of Love. The Arabic Part of Marriage is found by adding the Ascendant to the Descendant and subtracting Venus.

To have one's Sun, Moon, Venus, Ascendant Descendant or planet in or ruling the fifth or seventh house conjunct either of these Arabic Points in the other's chart is excellent for compatibility and romantic potential.

Transits, lunations or progressions to either of these Arabic Parts can bring on a relationship.

Tara met Sean when her progressed Moon was exactly conjunct her Arabic Part of Love, triggering the relationship.

The Arabic Part of Sudden Parting is found by adding the Ascendant to Saturn and subtracting Uranus.

The transiting Sun was in exact opposition to Tara's Arabic Part of Sudden Parting when she broke up with Sean. In addition, the transiting Full Moon in her natal fifth house was also conjunct it, ending the relationship.

The Arabic Part of Divorce is found by adding the Ascendant to Venus and subtracting the Descendant. A natal planet found here increases the probability of divorce, especially if it rules or is found in the fifth or seventh house.

An outer planet transit or progression negatively aspecting

this Arabic Part also increases the chances of divorce or separation.

Chapter 13

Midpoints

*M*idpoints have been used by astrologers since the thirteenth century. The principle lies in the theory that the half-way point between two planets, the Ascendant or Midheaven, is a sensitive point, where the energies of the two planets meet.

By using the table in the previous chapter, the following example can be followed to calculate a midpoint. A planet at 6 Aquarius and another at 12 Leo have a midpoint of 9 Taurus.

6 Aquarius	=	306°
+12 Leo	+	132°
	=	438°
	-	960°

(subtract 360° when the sum takes you over as the shorter midpoint is always taken)

	=	78°
divided by 2	=	39 or 9 Taurus

This midpoint can be activated by outer planet transits,

lunations or progressions to one or both charts.

Midpoints provide answers not only in predictions but in synastry. The most important midpoint is the Sun and Moon midpoint. For one's Venus to fall in the other's Sun/Moon would bring much compatibility and success potential. The Sun/Moon midpoints in favorable contact to each other is another testimony of romantic bliss.

Furthermore, a relationship has a good chance of working well if the Sun/Moon of one aspects the natal Sun or Moon of the other. Following in importance is the midpoint between Venus and Mars.

Tara met her first boyfriend at age seventeen when transiting Saturn was conjunct her Sun/Moon (both found in her seventh house of relationships). Also at this time transiting Jupiter was conjunct her Venus/Mars, planets of emotional and physical affections/interests.

Tara met her second boyfriend at age nineteen when the New Moon (beginnings and opportunities) was conjunct her Venus/Mars midpoint.

She met her third boyfriend at age twenty-two when transiting Saturn was in sextile to her Sun/Moon midpoint.

Other sensitive midpoints include the fifth and seventh house midpoint. By adding the sign and degree on both cusps and dividing the result by two this midpoint is determined. Naturally, it would be placed somewhere between the fifth and seventh house.

Transiting Venus or Mars passing through this midpoint can activate a relationship or romance.

Holly has Pluto in her natal fifth house and Jupiter in her natal seventh house. On the day she broke up with Greg, she moved from the east coast to the west coast after a terrible argument which took place when transiting Mars (arguments) was in exact conjunction to her Jupiter/Pluto (ruler of her fifth and seventh house) midpoint.

Chapter 14

Vertex

*T*he Vertex is a very sensitive and personal point in a chart indicating karmic or fated encounters as well as important events in relationships. It is always found between the fifth and the eighth house. It is also known as an "auxiliary Ascendant."

The Vertex has often been overlooked and does not receive the attention I believe it deserves, as much information can be gained from this point.

A natal planet conjunct or opposite the Vertex can reveal the type of relationships which attract us as well as the conditions. These events are triggered by outer planet transits, lunations and progressions to this point.

A natal fifth house Vertex shows a childlike nature in relationships. The need for fun and excitement from earlier years endures in relationships.

The Vertex found in the sixth house can bring the tendency to worry and criticize in relationships. The sense of duty is emphasized as well as the need for routine in relations.

The Vertex in the seventh indicates one who feels incomplete when not involved romantically with another. High expectations are likely within relationships.

An eighth house Vertex brings strong emotional tendencies when involved with another. Physical needs are strong and commitment is of utmost importance.

Expect a socially or romantically rewarding time when the new Moon or transiting or progressed Venus is conjunct the Vertex.

A break-up can coincide with a transiting planet in opposition or conjunction to the Vertex, such as a full Moon or transiting Mars, Saturn or Uranus.

By progressing the Vertex one degree per year after birth, you can determine when important or fateful relationships will enter your life by noting the aspects formed in the natal chart.

Tara has unfortunately had many failed relationships throughout the last ten years. She has Pluto conjunct her seventh house Vertex. Tara seems to repeat the same mistakes with all her boyfriends. She ends up losing control and feels tremendously hurt and betrayed when a relationship ends as she feels a part of her dies. This well exemplifies Scorpio, ruling sign of Pluto.

Her relationships are karmic and are meant to transform her. Until she learns to have control in a relationship, she will make the same mistakes over and over again.

Tara and Sean broke up while transiting Saturn was in opposition to her progressed Vertex. A five degree orb works best when applying transits to the progressed Vertex.

Tara met her first boyfriend when the progressed Vertex was conjunct her seventh house Moon. Another relationship which lasted five years commenced when the progressed Vertex was trine her natal Mars.

Christine and Brian met when the transiting North Node was exactly conjunct (activating) her natal seventh house

Vertex. Christine has an exact natal conjunction between the Vertex and Pluto. This conjunction triggered by the transiting North Node shows the beginning of a very karmic or fated relationship.

The Vertex is calculated as follows:

- Subtract the birth latitude from 90° (89°60"). This becomes the co-latitude.
- Under this new latitude, look up your natal Midheaven (MC) cusp as being the fourth house cusp in the table of houses. In other words, look under this co-latitude, the natal MC position as being the IC (fourth house) in the table of houses.
- The sign and degree on the Ascendant becomes the Vertex.

Chapter 15

Solar Returns

A solar return chart is cast for the date and time when the transiting Sun reaches the exact longitude it occupies in the natal chart each year. This date is found on or very close to the birthdate. Use the latitude and longitude of where you presently reside. The chart is valid until the next birthdate or when the Sun returns to the same longitude as it was at birth.

This type of chart is examined in the same manner as a natal chart. Solar return planets act as modifiers to the energy of the natal planets.

As outer planets are often in retrograde motion, they tend to become less personal or individual in terms of influence. The exception here is if an outer planet rules the solar first, fifth or seventh house. The inner planets are to be given more priority in solar return charts.

The house holding the solar return planet is by far more significant than the sign it occupies. The house is more personal and therefore specific in providing insight.

The Moon must be adjusted for the exact time of the solar return. The house holding the solar return Moon shows the area which will trigger the emotions throughout the year.

Many relationships are initiated when the Moon falls in the solar return fifth or seventh house. If found in the twelfth house, secret relations are likely as well as with one who is confined in some way, helpless or extremely dependent upon you, especially if Venus and/or Pluto is found in either of these houses forming a strong aspect.

A year of increased relationship potential is to be expected when the solar return Ascendant is the same sign and degree as the fifth or seventh natal house cusp.

The position of the solar return house Sun is the most important house to consider. The house holding the Sun shows where most of the activity throughout the year is to be expected.

If the Sun, Moon, Venus or Jupiter is found in the fifth house of your solar chart, it benefits relationships and results in increased romantic activity throughout the year. The more planets found in this house, the chances of relationship potentials are heightened.

However, do not despair if you are looking forward to a new or improved relationship this year and you do not have any planets in the solar fifth house.

Wherever Venus falls in the solar chart shows where or the type of relationships that one will be prone to attracting that year. For example, if Venus is found in the sixth house, it can result in a relationship with a coworker. The ninth house can bring romance while traveling or with a foreigner. Venus falling in the eleventh house can introduce romantic potentials through friendship. A twelfth house solar return Venus can bring a relationship of a secretive nature and so on.

Should Venus be retrograde in a solar return chart, it indicates a time of introspection and withdrawal. It is not the most fortunate time for personal relationships. It tends to bring the need for re-assessment in an existing romance. It can also activate a past relationship.

Venus falling in an intercepted solar return house either

manifests as limited romantic potential throughout the year or decreases the need for such activity. Secret relationships are also conducive to an intercepted Venus.

The Sun or Venus in the seventh house of a solar chart can cement an existing relationship. Remember, the fifth house is more a "fun" house in terms of romance and the seventh house is a "commitment" house.

The planets in a solar chart are examined within each other as well as to the planets in the natal chart. Transits and lunations again provide the timing of the triggering of solar return chart aspects. Transits to the angles of the solar return houses bring events which need to be dealt with. In relationship analysis, the seventh house is the most important angular house to examine.

The solar Ascendant moves approximately thirty degrees per month. The Moon moves (progresses) one degree per month. Tara broke up with Sean when her solar Ascendant moved to form a square to her natal Saturn. Her solar return progressed Moon formed a conjunction with her natal Mars, co-ruler of his Sun sign and Descendant.

To know if your calculations are correct, the Midheaven of the solar return chart moves ahead three signs each year. In other words, it remains in the same quadruplicity within three years. The Sun is always found in the same sign and degree as it is natally.

Christine met her current boyfriend through work. Her solar return chart for that specific year had Neptune as the ruler of the fifth house of romance, in trine to Saturn, the planet conjunct the sixth house cusp of work.

Chapter 16

Venus Returns

*T*he Venus return is the time of the year when this planet by transit, occupies the same sign and degree as in the natal chart, enhancing charm and popularity attracting people and romantic potentials. It is a good time to begin a new relationship as long as there are no heavy adverse transits also occurring. If already involved, it indicates improved relations.

A Venus return chart is cast for the exact time when transiting Venus occupies the same position it did at birth. Do not forget to adjust the Moon for time of the return. This type of chart can bring information regarding romances and their potential for the year ahead or until the next Venus return, as it provides deeper insight into relationships and the social life.

The first thing to consider is the position of Venus by house and the aspect(s) it receives. The house holding Venus reveals the area where its influence will be most felt and the aspects formed to this planet indicate the nature of this influence. Venus in the fifth or seventh house of a Venus return chart brings an active social or romantic year ahead.

Next to analyze are the natal and transiting planets of the Venus return chart and note if they conjunct an angular house (first, fourth, seventh, and tenth) as these strong energies will be most prominent during the coming year. For example, Tara had Venus in conjunction to the Midheaven of her Venus return chart one particular year. During this cycle she began a short-lived romance with her employer. Venus received several adverse aspects by transits as did the natal planets within the Venus return chart and therefore the relationship ended within a few months when it was triggered by a lunation. Venus in conjunction to the Midheaven can also bring social opportunities or valuable contacts within the career area.

In conjunction to the Ascendant, Venus rising also attracts many romantic potentials and socially rewarding opportunities for the year ahead. Any planet in conjunction to the Ascendant of this chart is also highly significant and should be examined as it will influence the social/romantic outlook and expression for the year ahead. Should this planet be Saturn, adverse aspects can bring increased relationship burdens or responsibility as well as break-ups, unrequited love and loneliness. Positive aspects can bring a solid, dependable, constructive, stable or past relationship to the chart owner. Uranus rising can bring a sudden unstable, indiscreet, idealistic or eccentric relationship under adverse aspects or bring a fresh, altruistic, exciting or platonic romance under positive transits.

In Christine's Venus return chart of one particular year, Venus was placed in the eleventh house of friends, hopes and wishes. During this cycle she met someone through a mutual friend whom she fell in love with. When transiting Saturn formed an opposition to Venus, the relationship broke up primarily because of this mutual friend who had first introduced them. As Venus remains as it did at birth, transiting Saturn would have opposed it whether a Venus return chart had been cast or not. What was learnt by this type of chart was that this relationship was initiated and destroyed by someone who was once a friend of the native as indicated by the eleventh house.

Chapter 17

Diurnal Chart

A diurnal (daily) chart is cast for a specific date in question. The natal figures remain the same, however substitute the natal sidereal time with the sidereal time of the chosen date.

Use the same latitude and longitude of birth and apply Daylight Time only if it was in effect at the time of birth. The Diurnal Ascendant will always be the same as the natal Ascendant on each birthdate.

This type of chart provides an incredible amount of insight when accompanied or triggered by transits, lunations and progressions. A diurnal chart also acts as a catalyst by pinpointing the exact date when a lunation or transit is triggered. A diurnal chart is of little value when examined by itself.

A diurnal chart cast for a specific date is therefore only applicable for twenty-four hours. The Midheaven in diurnal charts moves approximately a degree per day.

A quick method of these daily calculations makes it unnecessary to have to cast a chart every day. By totaling the natal figures without the natal sidereal time, the diurnal constant is determined and then added to the sidereal time of the date in question to arrive at the diurnal Ascendant. The rest of the houses fall as they do normally through the table of houses for the natal birth place.

To check your calculations, look to see where the transiting Sun falls in the diurnal chart. It should always fall in the same house of your natal chart as the same time is always used. If your natal Sun is very close to a natal house cusp, it could then fall in the house before or after the house holding your natal Sun.

If you arrive at a sidereal time giving the diurnal Ascendant as 16 Cancer and your natal Venus is placed at 20 Cancer, count down in the table of houses to how many days (four) it will take for the diurnal Ascendant to conjunct natal Venus. Four days after the diurnal Ascendant is 16 Cancer it will conjunct the natal Venus. This would be a day to expect romantic opportunities or events.

Examine the transits formed to the diurnal chart ruler as well as the aspects formed to the transiting diurnal chart ruler.

For example, with Leo on the Diurnal Ascendant, study the transits formed to your natal Sun as well as the aspects made between the transiting Sun and natal planets. The houses holding natal and transiting Sun are then activated.

Christine met her new boyfriend on the day when her diurnal Ascendant was conjunct her fifth house ruler. She split up with him a few months later but got back together with him when her diurnal Ascendant was sextile her natal Venus and was triggered by transiting Jupiter forming a trine to her natal Venus.

Transiting or natal Venus conjunct or well aspected to the diurnal Ascendant brings relationship benefits or opportunities. Adverse aspects between Venus and the diurnal Ascendant can result in troubles, setbacks or delays in relationship growth.

Tara's relationship came to an abrupt end when her diurnal Ascendant was in opposition to her natal Ascendant as well as transiting Venus, Mars and Uranus, her natal chart ruler.

Transiting or natal Saturn well aspected to the diurnal Ascendant can bring back a lover or at least bring contact with this person. An unfavorable aspect between Saturn and the diurnal Ascendant can break up a relationship or provide challenges which must be dealt with inside the relation.

Lunations are especially insightful with diurnals. New Moons provide opportunities and growth. Should a new Moon fall in the diurnal fifth or seventh house, or conjunct Venus or a planet in or ruling either of these houses, a favorable time in terms of romance can be expected.

A full Moon can, however, disrupt the social/romantic life, when found in the above mentioned conditions. This lunation can severe a relationship, especially when accompanied by other transits of the same nature.

Christine broke up with Dan when the full Moon fell in her diurnal fifth house of romance.

Chapter 18

Composite Chart

A composite chart is one which is composed of two charts. This new chart becomes the chart of the relationship itself.

The first step is to convert the Midheaven of both charts into 360 degrees, add them together and divide the sum by half. The result is then converted to sign and degree, becoming the composite Midheaven of the composite chart. The rest of the house cusps follow in order as they are listed in the table of houses for the latitude where the relationship is taking place.

Always take the shorter midpoint as it is stronger in influence. To always arrive at the shorter midpoint, subtract 360 degrees when the sum of both planets or points takes you over 360 degrees before dividing this sum in half.

The next step is to find the midpoint of the Sun, Moon, Mercury and so on in both charts until all are determined.

The cusp of the first house is determined by the composite Midheaven and the table of houses. However, by finding the midpoint of both Ascendants, a secondary composite Ascendant is determined and examined.

Transits, lunations and progressions are to be used as always in composite charts to time events. Consider what transits are being formed to planets in or ruling the composite fifth or seventh house.

Tara and Sean broke up when the detrimental full Moon was conjunct their composite seventh house Venus. Generally, a composite seventh house Venus would be ideal. However, this Venus was not only in opposition to both composite Ascendants but in square to composite Uranus and Pluto as well.

I have seen several break-ups when the full Moon transits through the composite seventh house of a couple's chart. However, the relationships that ended were not based on solid ground.

Composite charts provide much insight into compatibility as well. Further information can be derived in this area by calculating the midpoint of both Sun/Moon midpoints. Should this composite Sun/Moon midpoint aspect a natal Sun and/or Moon of one or both, compatibility is highly increased.

A composite chart can be progressed as you would a natal chart for insight into the direction a relationship is likely to take. Both charts are individually progressed for the same year and location where the relationship is taking place. Calculate the midpoint of both progressed Midheavens and follow as you did in the natal composite chart calculations to arrive at the progressed composite house cusp and planets.

The luck-bringers, transiting Venus and Jupiter, coming to a conjunction to the ruler of the composite fifth or seventh house of relationships brings opportunities for advancement in romantic matters.

The composite chart should be completely analyzed as the living entity the relationship is. A composite house holding three or more planets has strong emphasis on the relationship. For example, four planets in a composite ninth house of a couple would indicate much interest in either travel, cultures, foreign lands, higher learning, religion and spirituality.

The house holding the composite Sun and Moon is also of much importance. The Sun represents the personality of the relationship. For example the Sun in the composite third house will show a relationship that thrives on the interchange of thoughts and ideas. Both people relate to each other best through talking rather than through feelings and emotions.

The house holding the composite Moon shows how emotions are expressed in the relationship. For example, a composite Moon in the tenth house shows that both individuals thrive to get ahead in life together. One may help the other achieve occupational goals or social status. These goals bring each other emotional satisfaction and fulfillment.

The houses holding composite Venus and Mars are to be studied as well. For example, Venus in the composite first house shows a couple whose relationship is based on love and affection. This placement provides a powerful physical attraction between the two. The element of partnership is strong. This is an ideal place to have Venus in the composite chart of a couple.

The placement of Mars in the composite chart shows were most of the energy is concentrated. The house could provide clues as to where arguments are likely to arise.

Mars in the composite fifth house, for example, points toward conflicts arising through creative or social pursuits or interests. Much energy is expressed in terms of individuality and creativity. Each must give the other time to pursue personal interests.

The placing of Saturn in a composite chart is to be analyzed as it provides clues to as to where fears and insecurities lie within the relationship.

A well-placed (by aspect) Saturn would show reliability and endurance in the relationship. An adverse Saturn can show were restrictions and limitations are found in the relationship.

Saturn found in the composite second house of a couple's chart shows financial and material insecurity within the relationship. Monetary matters are a source of worry and concern to the chart owners. There is a fear of over-spending which can result in the inability to enjoy splurging occasionally. But each should remember that being overly conservative and cautious with finances can make one miss out on the finer things in life.

Chapter 18

Relationship Chart

*T*his type of chart is calculated by taking the halfway points between the birthdate, year and time of birth of two people. This is found by adding both dates and dividing by two. Repeat this calculation with both years, then with both times of birth. The latitude and longitude used is that where the relationship is occurring.

This chart represents the relationship itself as does a composite chart. Examine the transits and lunations formed to planets in the relationship chart for insight into the nature and direction this couple is likely to take together.

We will work with the relationship chart of Tara and Sean. It is interesting to see that the Ascendant of this relationship chart is the same sign and degree of Tara's natal Ascendant. While his natal Sun and rising sign were found intercepted in the relationship chart containing no planets, this is interpreted as meaning that this relationship meant much more to Tara than it did to Sean.

On the day they met, the following transits to their relationship chart were in effect:

- Tranisting Venus (romance) trine (rewarding) fifth house (love affair) Mercury
- transiting Mars (physical attraction) conjunct (powerful) seventh house (relationship) Mars (desire).
- Transiting Jupiter (luck/opportunity) trine (benefiting) fifth house Venus (courtship/affections)
- Transiting Pluto (intense emotions) conjunct (augmenting) Mercury, ruler of the fifth house (relationship/romance)
- Transiting Quarter Moon exactly conjunct (accentuating) seventh house Moon, triggering emotions within each other for each other

The aspects in this chart were all very promising. Saturn in this chart is in the first house, showing the ten year difference in age between the two. Tara, represented by the first house, was ten years older than Sean, represented by the seventh house. Saturn formed an opposition to Mars, Uranus and Pluto in the seventh house. This indicates a troubled relationship, which indeed it was as they constantly argued.

Venus was placed in the fifth house of Gemini. This showed that they shared many fun and happy times together as both were very social and fun-loving people.

Mars was conjunct Uranus (the chart ruler) and Pluto in Virgo in the seventh house. This revealed many arguments (Pluto) resulting from his (seventh house) critical (Virgo) nature. All this affected her deeply as these planets were square the Sun, her natal Sun sign ruler.

When they broke up, the following transits to the relationship chart were in effect:

- Transiting Venus (affection and romance) retrograde (reversals) in opposition (working against) to the Descendant (relationship)
- Transiting North Node square (obstacles/challenges) the Sun (seventh house relationship ruler) and conjunct (emphasizing) the North Node in the fourth house of

endings

- Transiting North Node conjunction Pluto (also representing endings) in the seventh house of relationships
- Transiting Saturn inconjunct (obstacles/separation) the seventh house Pluto—Pluto is also the ruler of the Scorpio Midheaven (reputation) of this relationship chart, affecting its status by ending it
- Full Moon (detrimental effect) conjunct (intensifying its effect) Venus (affections) in the fifth house (relationships)

Chapter 20

Horary Chart

*H*orary charts are based on the philosophy that the time a question is asked and becomes strongly imprinted in the mind, the heavens contain the answer. A chart is then cast for that specific time, which provides the answer to the question sought. The question posed must be clear and precise in order to accurately determine the outcome.

The chart is then cast as you would a natal chart, with the birth time being the exact time the question was asked. The latitude and longitude used is that of where the question was being asked.

Following are rules and guidelines to follow when analyzing and interpreting a horary chart.

Once the chart is cast, should you arrive at an Ascendant of three degrees or less, the chart is premature. It is too soon to determine the outcome of the matter. Should it be placed at twenty seven or more degrees, the question does not need answering because it is irrelevant and therefore too late; the result is already known.

Should the Moon in the horary chart be void of course, the matter is frozen and an answer is not available now. The

Moon must form at least one aspect with another planet in the horary chart for an event to transpire and be interpreted. The Moon is the secondary ruler or co-significator of the querent (person posing the question).

The first ruler is the planet closest to the first house cusp. If there is none, the ruler of the first house (Ascendant) is taken as the primary ruler or significator. This represents the querent (the inquirer).

If you are reading for yourself, you are represented by the first house. If Saturn falls in the first house, the chart is not fit to be read and your judgment may be clouded. If you are reading for another, the astrologer is represented by the seventh house. Should Saturn (obstruction) fall in the seventh house, the chart is not fit to be read.

Remember, although you the astrologer are actually posing the question, it is the querent who is represented by the Moon and Ascendant (it is their question) while you are represented by the seventh house.

An adverse aspect between Saturn and the Moon tends to indicate a delay regarding the outcome of the question. The Moon placed in the first house shows uncertainty on the part of the querent. Venus placed in this house shows a favorable outcome to relationship questions.

The first planet forming an aspect to the significators shows what is first to be expected. Should it be Jupiter, luck can be anticipated, or if it be Neptune, expect misunderstandings or uncertainty. The last planet making an aspect to the significators shows the end of the matter. Should it be a retrograde planet, the matter will not turn out as hoped.

If the first aspect made to the significators is a fortunate one but the last aspect made is not, the matter starts off well but does not end as planned. The reverse is to be interpreted if the first aspect made is unfavorable, but the last one is favorable.

Note the ruler of the fifth or seventh house for insight into relationship questions. The fifth house is regarded as the relationship itself and the seventh house represents the romantic partner. The partner is known as the quesited.

Should the ruler of the fifth or seventh house be retrograde, the partner may be hesitant in fully committing to this relationship, at least for now.

A promising outcome is to be expected if the Moon and/or significator is well-aspected and applying (approaching) to the ruler or planet in the fifth or seventh house.

Should the ruler of the fifth or seventh house be retrograde and applying to the ruler of the first house, the individual will likely become a lover or this person will come back to the querent if the relationship previously ended.

Note what aspects (if any) are being formed between the ruler of the querent (you) and the quesited (other) when asking questions about a relationship. The aspect provides clues as to the present state of the relationship.

Should these two planets, representing the couple, be in mutual reception (for example, Mars in Virgo and Mercury in Aries within a six degree orb) a positive outcome is to be expected. Should these two planets be negatively aspected to each other and/or other planets, friction, trouble, delays or separation are likely.

Events will transpire when both these significators are within aspect to each other. This is emphasized if the aspect becomes complete (exact) before either planet forms an aspect to another planet.

If one of the planets goes retrograde before the aspect is complete, the individual represented by that significator will back down, change his or her mind, or the event will take a radical turn and will not come to be.

If either or both of the significators are retrograde, the matter will not reach its fullest desire or potential.

If the significators are not involved in an aspect to each other, or if they are separating from an aspect, the event will not transpire as hoped. Promise is only indicated when the significators are applying and well-aspected to each other.

If before the significators form a perfect aspect one of the planets changes signs, it denotes a change before completion. The nature of this adjustment is seen by whether the aspect is favorable or not.

When Christine came to me years ago asking if I would be able to tell her if she would reunite with Dan, I immediately cast a horary chart for the time the question was posed.

The ruler of the empty fifth house (Dan/quesited) was Mercury. Mercury in Leo was applying to trine Venus, ruler of her first house. This would indicate a hopeful outcome. However, four days later Mercury would turn retrograde and would not complete the exact trine aspect to Venus. This changes the delineation completely. The couple never did get back together.

If the question sought is if the male querent will marry, analyze the Ascendant ruler, Moon and Venus. Should there be a favorable aspect between these planets and/or ruler of the first house, the outcome is hopeful. If the querent is a female, study the ruler of the Ascendant, Sun and Mars instead. If these two planets do not form an aspect, the answer is likely to be a negative one.

Samantha came to me inquiring about the probability of become involved with a specific person. She was represented by the Sun, having Leo placed in an empty first house. Her new interest was shown by Jupiter, placed in the seventh house. The Sun is the querent, Jupiter is the quesited. These two planets are applying to form a conjunction. The outcome is promising. Should the Sun have formed a negative aspect to another planet before it exactly came to conjunct Jupiter, the matter would have been obstructed and a relationship between these two people would not have been likely. Samantha did end up becoming involved with this man.

To find out if your lover is currently faithful, analyze the ruler of the seventh (the quesited) to see if it forms a fortunate aspect to any planet except the ruler of the first (you/querent). If it does, the lover is likely unfaithful and has another.

To find out if your partner/spouse will return to you. Note the ruler of the seventh house (spouse). A positive outcome is to be expected if this planet is retrograde and applying to form a fortunate aspect to the ruler of the first house (you/querent). The same can be expected if the Moon is applying to form a fortunate aspect to the Ascendant ruler.

Chapter 21

Your Ideal Companion

*I*n a male chart, the ideal companion is indicated by the planet to which his natal first Moon applies, as this planet represents the qualities sought in a partner. In the chart of a female, the same is indicated by the planet to which her natal first Sun applies, as this planet represents the qualities sought in a partner. This rule applies to same-sex relationships as well. For example, in the chart of male with the Moon first applying to aspect Uranus, the spouse or partner will display an Uranian/Aquarian temperament or personality. The aspect further provides clues to this nature. If the Moon first applies to form a trine to Jupiter, she will possess the positive attributes of Jupiter/Sagittarius such as optimism, generosity and humor while being open-minded and fun-loving. In the chart of a female, if the Sun first applies to form a square to Neptune, her companion will exhibit negative traits of Neptune/Pisces as being somewhat illusive, hypersensitive, indecisive, impractical and prone to escapism.

If there are no planets applying to either the Moon in a male chart or the Sun in the female chart, marriage or its equivalent may be delayed or is not that important to the individual.

In the chart of a male or female, Sun or Venus with Saturn aspects can indicate a partner that is of an age difference. An older partner is also indicated when one has the Sun or Venus in Capricorn or has this sign ruling the seventh house. A younger partner is often selected by those who have Sun or Venus in the youthful signs Gemini or Leo or have these signs ruling the fifth and/or seventh houses. When the ruler of the seventh house is positioned in the ninth house or the reverse, it tends to attract foreign partners or important relationships while abroad. A planet in the seventh house generally indicates the type of individual ideally suited. The more planets in this house, the more important relationships the native will have. The same applies to the number of aspects that are formed to the ruler of the seventh house of long-term relationships.

Sun signs must be compatible by element as the best relationships are generally found when Sun signs are in the same element of fire, earth, air or water. Fire and air signs work well together as do earth and water signs, as seen by the compatibility of opposite Sun signs. As mentioned in the Synastry chapter, one's Ascendant in the other's Sun sign and one's Moon in the same sign as the other's Sun are excellent for compatibility, particularly if in conjunction. Ascendants being in opposite signs is also conducive to long-term compatibility.

Early marriages are indicated with those who have water signs rising as do those born under a waxing Moon. In the chart of a female, the Sun found above the horizon tends to indicate early marriage as does the Moon in the chart of a male. The Moon afflicted by the Sun in the chart of a male, or Saturn afflicting his Moon or Venus can also bring delays or a reluctance to marry. In a female chart, the same applies if the Sun is afflicted by the Moon, or Saturn is afflicting her Sun or Venus. Uranus in the seventh house in the chart of a male or female tends to prevent marriage unless the Moon (in a male chart) or the Sun (in a female chart) first applies to the benefic planets Venus and/or Jupiter.

Divorce is indicated by having an afflicted Uranus in the seventh house, particularly by Venus, as the need for freedom and independence is great. Uranus in conjunction to the seventh house ruler can also bring divorce. In a male chart, the Moon afflicted by Uranus is indicative of divorce as is the Sun afflicted by Uranus in the chart of a female. Second marriages are often formed by those with Gemini, Virgo, Sagittarius or Pisces rising. This is also indicated by the Moon in a male chart or the Sun in the female chart found in either of these mutable signs and applying to form more than one major aspect to other planets.

When Venus is afflicted by Saturn of either a male or female chart, one must work harder at having positive, fulfilling relationships. The natal Moon found in the last three degrees of a sign can also bring marital delays or a lack of interest. Should the ruler of the seventh house form an adverse aspect to Saturn, or Saturn itself be found in the seventh house with hard aspects particularly to the seventh house ruler, late or no marriage will likely take place due to a fear of being burdened or saddled with too much responsibility.

It is important to remember that none of these rules are strong enough alone to bring about the results indicated. At least three of these aspects or placings are necessary to bring about the effects delineated.

In esoteric Astrology, karmic indicators show unresolved ties left over from past lives. The Lunar Nodes are indicative of our karmic past conditions as they are meeting points between the Earth, Sun and Moon. A planet in one's chart in conjunction to the other's North Node or Dragon's Head, shows a previous positive relationship where rewards can now be experienced. If a planet conjuncts the other's South Node or Dragon's Tail, unresolved problems that existed in the past resurface and requiring handling in order to progress.

Saturn is the planet ruling karma and one's inner planet

(Sun through Mars) in conjunction to the other's Saturn can also bring about a karmic relationship, particularly if the twelfth house of past lives or its ruler is also involved.

Chapter 22

Closing

I hope to have succeeded in my goal of providing you with several methods of answering romance and relationship questions.

We are inclined to pick up a book such as this when we are either lonely, going through rough times in a relationship or have just broken up with another. We tend not to question matters when they are going well.

I feel that at this point it is imperative to mention that one should never lose oneself through or because of another. You are on the wrong path of life if your emotional well-being depends upon another. Should you have recently been hurt by a relationship, accept the loss, allow yourself the time to grieve and give yourself plenty of affection, encouragement and credit for trying in order to begin the healing process.

Make a list if you have to of the qualities you are looking for in another. I have known this technique to work for several friends and clients who shortly therafter met someone possessing the traits on the wish list. You must know exactly what you want in life in order to be able to achieve it.

If the stars point toward you being single for a certain

amount of time, use this break to expand your interests, set goals, pamper and rediscover yourself. The time will soon come when the heavens will unite you with another. By using the techniques in this book, you will already know when this time will eventually find you.

Each and every relationship we go through is meant to be a learning experience. Look back, think hard and analyze what each past relationship has taught you. Use this experience to grow and to learn how to avoid repeating negative patterns or mistakes in the future. Never take all the blame when a relationship fails. It takes two to make a relationship and it takes two to break a relationship.

I wish you all the luck and success in your relationship studies, research, pursuits, adventures, experiences and quests!

Ana Ruiz